G000071390

SPORTING GREATS

SPORTING GREATS

Summersdale Publishers Ltd
46 West Street
Chichester
West Sussex
PO19 1RP
UK

www.summersdale.com

Printed and bound in the Czech Republic

ISBN: 978-1-84953-861-9

Substantial discounts on bulk quantities of Summersdale books are available to corporations, professional associations and other organisations. For details contact Nicky Douglas by telephone: +44 (0) 1243 756902, fax: +44 (0) 1243 786300 or email: nicky@summersdale.com.

SPORTING GREATS

THE WIT AND WISDOM OF TOP-CLASS LEGENDS

RICHARD BENSON

summersdale

Sport is a universal language,
building more bridges
between people than
anything else I can think of.

SEBASTIAN COE

Float like a butterfly,
sting like a bee.

MUHAMMAD ALI

In 1969 I gave up women and alcohol – it was the worst 20 minutes of my life.

GEORGE BEST

IT'S NOT WHETHER
YOU WIN OR LOSE – BUT
WHETHER I WIN OR LOSE.

SANDY LYLE

The road to Easy
Street goes through
the sewer.

JOHN MADDEN

Some people want it to happen, some wish it would happen, others make it happen.

MICHAEL JORDAN

I'll let the racket do
the talking.

JOHN McENROE

You miss 100 per cent
of the shots you
don't take.

WAYNE GRETZKY

LOOKING FOR
PERFECTION IS THE
ONLY WAY TO
MOTIVATE YOURSELF.

RONNIE O'SULLIVAN

If you don't have the balls to brake late, that's your problem.

LEWIS HAMILTON

We had a good team on paper. Unfortunately, the game was played on grass.

BRIAN CLOUGH

Some dreams do come true.

BRADLEY WIGGINS

You need fear and doubt to drive you on. Without it, you end up living in the past.

TONY McCOY

For myself, losing is not
coming second. It's getting
out of the water knowing
you could have done better.

IAN THORPE

When you have confidence,
you can have a lot of fun.
And when you have fun, you
can do amazing things.

JOE NAMATH

I ALWAYS BELIEVED THAT
SKIING WAS SOMETHING
SERIOUS, THAT IT WAS
A WAY OF LIVING A
WHOLE LIFE.

JEAN-CLAUDE KILLY

You always want to
test yourself against
the best.

DAVID BECKHAM

Happiness is a long
walk with a putter.

GREG NORMAN

I have never tried to compare myself to anyone else.

SACHIN TENDULKAR

If you want to be the best, you have to do things that other people aren't willing to do.

MICHAEL PHELPS

IF THE STABLE GATE
IS CLOSED, CLIMB
THE FENCE.

JULIE KRONE

Champions keep playing until they get it right.

BILLIE JEAN KING

I think it's a great idea to talk during sex, as long as it's about snooker.

STEVE DAVIS

Don't dream of winning. Train for it!

MO FARAH

I'm a full-blooded racer.
What do people think we are
here for, a Sunday outing?

MICHAEL SCHUMACHER

The best decisions aren't
made with your mind,
but with your instincts.

LIONEL MESSI

Focus on remedies, not faults.

JACK NICKLAUS

EACH HAKA HAS ITS
OWN INTERPRETATION
BUT YOU HAVE TO
MAKE SURE YOU ARE
IN UNISON WITH
YOUR TEAMMATES.

JONAH LOMU

If you want to run, run a mile.
But if you want to experience
another life, run a marathon.

EMIL ZÁTOPEK

Never let the fear of striking out get in your way.

BABE RUTH

A champion is
someone who gets
up when he can't.

JACK DEMPSEY

Just go out there
and do what you
have to do.

MARTINA NAVRATILOVA

THE MORE DIFFICULT
THE VICTORY, THE
GREATER THE HAPPINESS
IN WINNING.

PELÉ

Enjoy the journey, enjoy
every moment, and
quit worrying about
winning and losing.

MATT BIONDI

Cycling is my job but it
also feels spiritual and
connected and it's all
I ever wanted to do.

CHRIS FROOME

**If you only ever give
90 per cent in training
then you will only ever give
90 per cent when it matters.**

MICHAEL OWEN

I look into their eyes,
shake their hand, pat
their back, and wish them
luck, but I am thinking,
'I am going to bury you.'

SEVE BALLESTEROS

If it's difficult, I'll do it now. If it's impossible, I'll do it presently.

DON BRADMAN

I play with a fear of letting people down. That's what motivates me.

JONNY WILKINSON

SCIENTISTS HAVE
PROVEN THAT IT'S
IMPOSSIBLE TO LONG-
JUMP 30 FEET, BUT I
DON'T LISTEN TO THAT
KIND OF TALK.

CARL LEWIS

Concentration and
mental toughness are
the margins of victory.

BILL RUSSELL

Just believe in yourself.
Even if you don't, pretend
that you do and, at
some point, you will.

VENUS WILLIAMS

Half the game is
mental; the other half
is being mental.

Winning is everything. The only ones who remember you when you come second are your wife and your dog.

DAMON HILL

AS LONG AS I BREATHE,
I ATTACK.

BERNARD HINAULT

Enjoy your golf and smell the roses along the way. Golf is supposed to be a lot of fun.

LAURA DAVIES

Being fit is an investment for the future.

REBECCA ADLINGTON

My proudest achievement
is producing my daughter.
Then sailing round the world.

ROBIN KNOX-JOHNSTON

When people succeed,
it is because of hard
work. Luck has nothing
to do with success.

DIEGO MARADONA

I want to stress again one aspect of the game which is most important. Never argue with an umpire.

IAN BOTHAM

Everyone's dream
can come true if you
just stick to it and
work hard.

SERENA WILLIAMS

WHEN I LOST MY
DECATHLON WORLD
RECORD, I TOOK IT LIKE
A MAN. I ONLY CRIED
FOR TEN HOURS.

DALEY THOMPSON

Rhythm is everything in boxing. Every move you make starts with your heart, and that's in rhythm or you're in trouble.

SUGAR RAY ROBINSON

Forget what is behind
and press toward what
is ahead, toward the
goal to win the prize.

BETSY KING

Worrying gets you nowhere.
If you turn up worrying
about how you're going to
perform, you've already lost.

USAIN BOLT

One man can be a crucial ingredient on a team, but one man cannot make a team.

KAREEM ABDUL-JABBAR

A MAN WHO WINS
IS A MAN WHO
THINKS HE CAN.

ROGER FEDERER

It's been a long journey grafting and grafting, but anything is possible.

MO FARAH

I've never played for a
draw in my life.

ALEX FERGUSON

The first thing is to be patient, which is probably the hardest thing to do.

SHANE WARNE

Friendships born on the field
of athletic strife are the
real gold of competition.
Awards become corroded,
friends gather no dust.

JESSE OWENS

Smile well and often. It makes people wonder what you're up to.

LEROY 'SATCHEL' PAIGE

Ability may get you
to the top, but it takes
character to keep
you there.

JOHN WOODEN

AN OTHERWISE HAPPILY
MARRIED COUPLE MAY
TURN A MIXED DOUBLES
GAME INTO A SCENE
FROM *WHO'S AFRAID OF
VIRGINIA WOOLF?*

ROD LAVER

There are two things no man will admit he can't do well: drive and make love.

STIRLING MOSS

When you're riding, only
the race in which you're
riding is important.

BILL SHOEMAKER

The things you learn from sports – setting goals, being part of a team, confidence – that's invaluable.

SUMMER SANDERS

Experience is a great advantage. The problem is that when you get the experience, you're too damned old to do anything about it.

JIMMY CONNORS

I STILL DON'T THINK THIS
500 MAKES ME A GREAT
CRICKETER. I'VE STILL
MUCH TO LEARN.

BRIAN LARA ON SCORING
501 RUNS IN 1994

Anyone can be clever;
the trick is not to think
the other guy is stupid.

JOSÉ MOURINHO

The whole point of
rugby is that it is, first
and foremost, a state
of mind, a spirit.

JEAN-PIERRE RIVES

I was 12 when I started out
and 34 before I achieved
my dream. That should
give people hope.

KELLY HOLMES

They should send Borg
away to another planet.
We play tennis. He plays
something else.

ILIE NĂSTASE

It's the iron in the mind, not in the supplements, that wins medals.

STEVE REDGRAVE

The water is your friend...
Just share the same
spirit as the water, and
it will help you move.

ALEXANDER POPOV

I DO SWEAR A LOT, BUT
THE ADVANTAGE IS
THAT HAVING PLAYED
ABROAD, I CAN CHOOSE
A DIFFERENT LANGUAGE
FROM THE REFEREE'S.

JÜRGEN KLINSMANN

The decathlon? Nine
Mickey Mouse events
and a 1,500 metres.

STEVE OVETT

You are only as good
as your last game.

IAN BOTHAM

This is the second most exciting indoor sport, and the other one shouldn't have spectators.

DICK VERTLEIB ON BASKETBALL

Your body is your
temple. You do your
body good, your body
will do you good.

FLOYD MAYWEATHER JR

IT WAS LIKE AN ALIEN
ABDUCTION OUT THERE.
SOMEONE INVADED HIS
BODY AND TURNED HIM
INTO THE GREATEST
VOLLEYER IN THE
UNIVERSE.

JIM COURIER ON LOSING
TO TIM HENMAN

To be at the top of my sport
you have to have that killer
instinct and when I'm at
the table I'm an animal.

STEPHEN HENDRY

If everything seems under control, you're just not going fast enough.

MARIO ANDRETTI ON MOTOR RACING

Training can be monotonous,
and it is hard work, but
you never lose sight of
why you are doing it.

CHRIS HOY

In racing, to insult a
man's horse is worse
than insulting his wife.

JOHN OAKSEY

I believe the target of anything in life should be to do it so well that it becomes an art.

ARSÈNE WENGER

If you fail to prepare, you're prepared to fail.

MARK SPITZ

WINNING IS A HABIT.
UNFORTUNATELY, SO
IS LOSING.

VINCE LOMBARDI

The day it arrives, it will arrive. It could be today or 50 years later. The only sure thing is that it will arrive.

AYRTON SENNA ON DEATH, NOT LONG BEFORE HIS FATAL CRASH

Tennis is a perfect
combination of violent action
taking place in an atmosphere
of total tranquillity.

BILLIE JEAN KING

Throwing a fastball by Hank
Aaron is like trying to sneak
the sunrise past a rooster.

CURT SIMMONS

Everything is practice.

PELÉ

NO MATTER HOW
GOOD YOU GET YOU
CAN ALWAYS GET
BETTER AND THAT'S
THE EXCITING PART.

TIGER WOODS

As an athlete the
Olympics are the
ultimate competition.

JESSICA ENNIS-HILL

Use every weapon
within the rules and
stretch the rules to
breaking point.

FRED TRUEMAN

Some people think football is
a matter of life and death...
I can assure them it is much
more serious than that.

BILL SHANKLY

I became a great runner
because if you're a kid in
Leeds and your name is
Sebastian you've got to
become a great runner.

SEBASTIAN COE

If you give 100 per cent all of the time, somehow things will work out in the end.

LARRY BIRD

If you aren't going all the way, why go at all?

JOE NAMATH

I THREW THE KITCHEN
SINK AT HIM BUT
HE WENT TO THE
BATHROOM AND
GOT HIS TUB.

ANDY RODDICK ON ROGER FEDERER

It really is all about believing in yourself: 80 per cent mental, 20 per cent physical.

VICTORIA PENDLETON

There may be people
that have more talent
than you, but there's no
excuse for anyone to work
harder than you do.

DEREK JETER

I push myself to
be the best I can be.
I don't worry about what
other people are doing.

ANNIKA SÖRENSTAM

Success is a process...
Sometimes there are
stones thrown at you,
and you convert them
into milestones.

SACHIN TENDULKAR

I LOVE THE WINNING,
I CAN TAKE THE LOSING,
BUT MOST OF ALL
I LOVE TO PLAY.

BORIS BECKER

An athlete cannot run with money in his pockets. He must run with hope in his heart and dreams in his head.

EMIL ZÁTOPEK

I've failed over and over
and over again in my life,
and that is why I succeed.

MICHAEL JORDAN

If you don't believe you
can make every putt,
why bother trying?

ERNIE ELS

Whoever said 'It's not whether you win or lose that counts' probably lost.

MARTINA NAVRATILOVA

If I had to make the choice
between staying married
and playing snooker,
snooker would win.

RAY REARDON

The man who can drive
himself further once the
effort gets painful is the
man who will win.

ROGER BANNISTER

THE REASON OF FOOTBALL IS NOT TO BE THE BEST BUT TO BE THE BEST TEAM.

BARRY SANDERS

It is not always possible
to be the best, but it is
always possible to improve
your own performance.

JACKIE STEWART

A good hockey player plays where the puck is. A great hockey player plays where the puck is going to be.

WAYNE GRETZKY

Set your goals high,
and don't stop till
you get there.

BO JACKSON

Losing makes me even more motivated.

SERENA WILLIAMS

THERE IS NOTHING
MORE EXCITING IN
SPORT WHEN THE TOP
TWO COUNTRIES IN THE
WORLD ARE BATTLING
FOR THE ASHES.

IAN BOTHAM

Anyone who sacrifices
his dreams to reality is
forever beaten.

THOMAS MÜLLER

Negative thoughts
lead to poor shots.

LAURA DAVIES

I just imagine all the other
runners are big spiders, and
then I get super scared.

USAIN BOLT

Looking too far ahead
can be distracting.

CHRIS HOY

Grand Prix driving is like
balancing an egg on a spoon
while shooting the rapids.

GRAHAM HILL

It is not the size of a
man but the size of his
heart that matters.

EVANDER HOLYFIELD

IT NEVER GETS EASIER,
YOU JUST GO FASTER.

GREG LeMOND

When I go out and race,
I'm not trying to beat
opponents, I'm trying to
beat what I have done.

IAN THORPE

You don't fear for your life
in the middle of a storm –
you can't really afford to.

ELLEN MacARTHUR

You need to play with
supreme confidence, or else
you'll lose again, and then
losing becomes a habit.

JOE PATERNO

I wouldn't say I was the best manager in the business. But I was in the top one.

BRIAN CLOUGH

I DON'T GIVE UP.
NEVER HAVE.
NEVER WILL.

JONAH LOMU

When I said, 'You're a
disgrace to mankind,' I was
talking to myself, not you.

JOHN McENROE
TO A WIMBLEDON UMPIRE

It's all about the journey, not the outcome.

CARL LEWIS

Every ball is for me the
first ball, whether my score
is 0 or 200, and I never
visualise the possibility of
anybody getting me out.

DON BRADMAN

I have always thought I was
the best ever player. I have
never looked at another
player and felt inferior.

GEORGE BEST

If you don't practise
you don't deserve
to win.

ANDRE AGASSI

Part of the art of bowling
spin is to make the batsman
think something special is
happening when it isn't.

SHANE WARNE

PLAYING THE GAME,
REPRESENTING THE TEAM,
GIVING MY ALL AND
NEVER LETTING GO HAS
MEANT EVERYTHING
TO ME.

JONNY WILKINSON

Be strong in body,
clean in mind, lofty
in ideals.

JAMES NAISMITH

I don't focus on what I'm up against. I focus on my goals and I try to ignore the rest.

VENUS WILLIAMS

If someone is not nervous,
I am not sure what sport
they are involved in.

BRIAN LARA

A lot of snooker players
are too intense and serious.
I want to be like Billy the Kid.

RONNIE O'SULLIVAN

TO GIVE YOURSELF THE
BEST POSSIBLE CHANCE
OF PLAYING TO YOUR
POTENTIAL, YOU MUST
PREPARE FOR EVERY
EVENTUALITY. THAT
MEANS PRACTICE.

SEVE BALLESTEROS

I've always believed that you should never, ever give up and you should always keep fighting even when there's only a slightest chance.

MICHAEL SCHUMACHER

Cycling has given
me everything.

BRADLEY WIGGINS

You have to dream of
success to make it happen,
and if you don't believe in
yourself, nobody else will.

TONY McCOY

You can't put a limit on anything. The more you dream, the further you get.

MICHAEL PHELPS

It's not whether you get knocked down, it's whether you get up.

VINCE LOMBARDI

Have fun, because
that's what life is
all about.

RYAN LOCHTE

IT ISN'T THE MOUNTAINS
AHEAD TO CLIMB THAT
WEAR YOU OUT; IT'S THE
PEBBLE IN YOUR SHOE.

MUHAMMAD ALI

I hate to lose more than I love to win.

JIMMY CONNORS

If you don't have
confidence, you'll always
find a way not to win.

CARL LEWIS

Achievement is largely the product of steadily raising one's levels of aspiration and expectation.

JACK NICKLAUS

Desire is the most
important factor in the
success of any athlete.

BILL SHOEMAKER

YOU'VE GOT TO
CELEBRATE THE GOOD
DAYS BECAUSE THERE ARE
BRUTAL DAYS THAT MAKE
THE GOOD ONES SWEET.

BRIAN O'DRISCOLL

One chance is all you need.

JESSE OWENS

There are no traffic
jams along the
extra mile.

ROGER STAUBACH

It's hard to beat a person who never gives up.

BABE RUTH

If you're interested in finding out more
about our books, find us on Facebook at
Summersdale Publishers and follow
us on Twitter at @Summersdale.

www.summersdale.com